FEB 2 8 2018

NATIONS
and
NATIONALITY

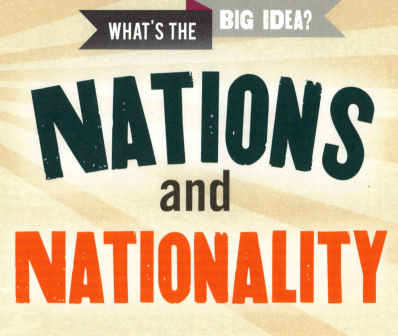

Tim Cooke

Cavendish
Square
New York

Published in 2018 by Cavendish Square Publishing, LLC
243 5th Avenue, Suite 136 New York, NY 10016

© 2018 Brown Bear Books Ltd

Website: cavendishsq.com

CPSIA compliance information: Batch #CS17CSQ:

All websites were available and accurate when this book went to press.

Library of Congress Cataloging-in-Publication Data

Names: Cooke, Tim.
Title: Nations and nationality / Tim Cooke.
Description: New York : Cavendish Square, 2018. | Series: What's the big idea?: a history of the ideas that shape our world | Includes index.
Identifiers: ISBN 9781502628206 (library bound) | ISBN 9781502628213 (ebook)
Subjects: LCSH: Nationalism--Juvenile literature. | Nationalities, Principle of.
Classification: LCC JC311.C66 2018 | DDC 320.54--dc23

For Brown Bear Books Ltd:
Managing Editor: Tim Cooke
Editorial Director: Lindsey Lowe
Designer: Supriya Sahai
Design Manager: Keith Davis
Children's Publisher: Anne O'Daly
Picture Manager: Sophie Mortimer

Manufactured in the United States of America

CONTENTS

INTRODUCTION

History has been shaped by the idea of nations and nationality. Although countries are similar to nations, they are not quite the same.

A nation is a group of people who share the same culture and traditions. A country or state, meanwhile, is a geographical and political area ruled by a single government. If a country is inhabited only by a single nation, it is sometimes called a nation-state.

From a young age, people are encouraged to feel loyal to the country where they live. Most people know their country's flag or national anthem. They take pride in being a citizen. They may take pleasure when their country's sports teams perform well or when someone from their country makes a contribution to science.

This is the crown of the Holy Roman Empire. The empire lasted from 800 until 1806. It included peoples with different languages and backgrounds. →

Americans declared their independence from Britain in 1776. The new country was a republic, making it different from the monarchies of Europe.

People probably know the name of their capital city, and perhaps who controls the government. By looking on a map, they can tell where the borders of their country are.

Difficult questions

In the past, the ideas of countries and nationality were very different. Until the 1800s, people's lives were shaped not by where they lived but by who ruled them. A sense of nationalism, or pride in one's country, began to grow in the early 1800s.

The idea of nationality raises many questions. Is everyone who lives in a country a citizen of that country? If a citizen disobeys the laws of his or her country are they still entitled to live there? And do changes in communications and international trade mean that countries are now outdated? Some people believe that we now live in an interconnected world.

WHAT IS A NATION?

Today, most of the world is divided into 195 nation-states, or countries. However, countries are relatively modern creations. For most of history they did not exist.

What defines a country might seem straightforward. A country is an area of land with clear geographical borders that is occupied by people who are governed under the same political system. A country's people usually speak the same language. They are united by a shared **culture** and history.

PHARAOH

The kings of Egypt ruled over one of the most powerful states in the ancient world. →

All the people who live inside a country are called citizens. This suggests that they are treated equally under the laws of the country. However, even this simple definition of a country has many problems.

Borders of countries can and have changed at various times. Countries have come under the control of other countries. **Immigration** means that the people who live in countries such as Britain or France no longer share a single culture or history. In some cases, **ethnic** groups within a country speak different languages than the majority of the people.

Peoples come together

The equivalents of modern nations in the past were widely varied. The first communities probably consisted of **extended families** or groups of families. They may have cooperated for protection or to make it easier to hunt for food. Communities learned to grow crops and settled on permanent sites.

TIMELINE

3200 BCE
Organized groups of people emerge in Mesopotamia and Egypt. They develop into powerful empires.

800s BCE
States begin to emerge on the islands and mainland of what is now Greece. These states are usually based on a powerful city that dominates the region.

27 BCE
The Roman Empire is founded. At its greatest extent, it controls most of Europe, the Mediterranean, and the Middle East.

As populations grew, competition increased for the best land and for **resources** such as water. Leaders emerged who offered to protect their people in return for being able to live a more privileged lifestyle. Groups clashed. Successful groups grew until they split and settled in another village or town.

Centers of power emerged in various regions. In Mesopotamia, modern-day Iraq, river mud provided material for building cities such as Ur, Sumer, and Babylon. Cities grew in power, claimed power over the entire region, then lost power to their neighbors. In Egypt, the Nile River became the focus of a civilization that flourished for around 3,000 years. Egypt's culture dominated the Nile Valley. Outside the Nile Valley, however, its borders were lost in the sands of the desert. In addition, some of the **dynasties**, or families, that ruled Egypt included foreigners from Nubia, Libya, and elsewhere.

ZIGGURAT

In Mesopotamia, people used mud from the river plains to make bricks. They built monuments, such as this **ziggurat** in Ur, in modern-day Iraq.

WARRIORS

The first emperor of China's Qin dynasty (221–206 BCE) used warfare to create a large empire. The emperor's tomb is guarded by an army of terra-cotta warriors.

←

Centers of power

From around 4,000 BCE, powerful states also emerged in the Yellow River Valley in China and on the Ganges Plain of modern India and Pakistan. These states sometimes conquered their neighbors and built **empires**, such as in Persia or Han China. Rulers unified their territories by creating armies and **bureaucracies**. Roads and other **infrastructure** helped unify their empires. Shared forms of writing, money, and weights and measures also made trading easier.

RISE OF CULTURES

The earliest areas where powerful cultures developed were spread around the world.

3200 BCE
MESOPOTAMIA, EGYPT

1600 BCE
CHINA

1200 BCE
AMERICAS

2000 BCE
AEGEAN

3000 BCE
INDUS VALLEY

In the 1000s BCE, most of the world was not part of an empire. It was divided into much smaller political units. Many of these units were kingdoms. They had a king or queen whose government controlled the immediate area. Often, the power of the government was weaker in areas farthest away from the heart of the kingdom. This created a shifting pattern where the influence of different kingdoms overlapped. In Buddhist Southeast Asia, this system of overlapping power centers was known as a "mandala."

The classical world

In Greece, peoples who shared the same language and culture began in the 800s BCE to form a series of different and often competing Greek states. The states were based on the islands and regions of the Greek peninsula. Although the Greeks shared similar culture and language, they were politically divided.

DAILY LIFE

This temple carving from India shows scenes of everyday life. Much of India and Southeast Asia were united by a common religion, Buddhism. →

COLOSSEUM

Wherever the Romans settled, they put up buildings like those in Rome. This amphitheater for gladiator fights was constructed in Tunisia in North Africa.

In contrast, the Romans who replaced the Greeks as the dominant power in the Mediterranean, came from different cultures but were united politically. From the 100s BCE their empire spread across Europe. The Romans gave all the people whose territory they conquered the right to call themselves citizens of Rome, regardless of their race.

At around the same time in North and South America, peoples developed an idea of nationality that was not based on land. They based it on shared languages, culture, and beliefs. Cultural groups inhabited similar landscapes, such as the plains or woodlands. The borders between their territories were only loosely defined.

IN SUMMARY

■ As societies developed, people formed large groups based on their shared cultural background and language.

■ Some successful early societies were able to control a wide area. They incorporated other peoples into a single, powerful empire.

TRIBES, EMPIRES, CITIES, AND KINGDOMS

The Roman empire grew so large it was almost impossible to govern. Its destruction began a period of change.

Rome was conquered in 476. The regions of its former empire fell under the rule of various European peoples, including the Goths, Huns, and Franks. As in previous centuries, these peoples had clear regions of influence but the borders between their territories were hazy or overlapping.

FRENCH HEROINE

Joan of Arc led French forces in the Hundred Years' War (1337–1453). She became an important national symbol for France.

A series of Germanic peoples migrated west into the former Roman empire. This caused a domino effect within Europe. Among the significant population shifts was that of the Angles and Saxons. These Germanic tribes began to move to the island of Britain in around 450 CE, a few decades after the Romans had left. Over the next centuries, the newcomers **assimilated** into the existing population. A new Anglo-Saxon culture emerged in Britain. By the 1000s, a clear English identity had also emerged, although Britain remained divided into separate kingdoms.

A European empire

In around 800 King Charlemagne of the Franks extended his territory from France to Italy and central and northern Europe, where peoples with the same language and cultural background lived under different rulers. By bringing these populations into his empire, Charlemagne laid the foundations for the development of what are now countries in France, the Low Countries, and Germany.

TIMELINE

476 The Roman Empire in the west is overthrown, marking the start of a period of widespread population movement.

800 The Frankish king Charlemagne creates an empire that covers much of France and central Europe. The state he creates paves the way for later nations to emerge.

1337 The Hundred Years' War begins between England and France. The 1300s mark an increase in nationalism among people in Europe.

The pope made Charlemagne Holy Roman Emperor in 800. That tied Europe closely to the Roman Catholic Church. At that time, the idea of Europe barely existed. Instead, Europeans saw themselves as belonging to Christendom, or the territory of the Christian church. In southeast Europe, the Byzantine Empire was based in Constantinople (modern-day Istanbul). The Byzantines practiced a different form of Christianity called Eastern Orthodox Christianity.

Christians and Muslims

Christendom became more strictly defined in the 1000s. An Islamic empire had developed in the Middle East since the 600s. It seemed to threaten the borders of Christian territory. Europeans went to the Holy Land to fight Muslims in wars called the **Crusades**. The crusaders had some success but were finally defeated. Internally, too, Christendom felt threatened. An Islamic advance into France from Spain was stopped in 732 by the Frankish leader Charles Martel.

EMPEROR

Charlemagne kneels before the pope as a sign of the authority of the church. The Christian faith was key to shaping Europe in the Middle Ages.

→

HOLY CITY

Christian crusaders conquer Jerusalem in 1099. Europeans ruled the city for nearly 200 years. It was recaptured by Muslim forces in 1291.

NEW COUNTRIES

Large Jewish populations in Europe were seen as a threat by many Europeans. In 1290, King Edward I expelled Jews from England. In eastern Europe, Christian knights launched the Crusades against the last non-Christian, or pagan, populations.

The defeat of the Crusades weakened the Roman Catholic Church in Europe. In place of the authority of the church, **nationalism** became more important.

Many modern countries were formed during the Middle Ages (their names were sometimes different).

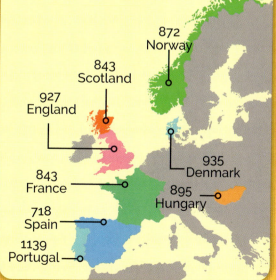

872 Norway

843 Scotland

927 England

935 Denmark

843 France

895 Hungary

718 Spain

1139 Portugal

Most land was owned by monarchs, who distributed it to nobles in return for support. Kingship was passed on through family lines known as dynasties. As dynasties gained or lost power, their kingdoms grew or shrank. A family might own territory in what are now different countries, and rule different peoples.

The emergence of nationalism

In 1066, the Norman prince William defeated England's King Harold I and took the English throne. The English were an assimilation of Britons, Romans, Angles, and Saxons. The Normans who arrived in England with William brought another addition to the national identity.

In 1337, disputes between British and French rulers about territory in France led to the Hundred Years' War (in fact, it lasted until 1453).

TAPESTRY

The Bayeux Tapestry is a contemporary depiction of the Battle of Hastings. William defeated King Harold I, who died in the battle.

During the long conflict, England's noble knights probably shared more of a common culture with the French knights they fought than with the English peasants who fought alongside them.

This was the period when nationalism began to emerge. Bonds of ethnicity or community united peoples. These developments were strongest in states with clear borders, such as England, France, Spain, and Portugal. National heroes emerged whose deeds celebrated **patriotism**. They included the English King Alfred, who led resistance to the Vikings, and Joan of Arc in France. Elsewhere, in the early 1300s William Tell became a hero of Swiss nationalism.

WILLIAM TELL

The Swiss told stories about how William Tell helped free them from Austrian rule. In this illustration, Tell and his son have killed a monstrous beast. →

IN SUMMARY

■ The Middle Ages saw the disappearance of the Roman Empire and, later, the weakening of the Catholic Church after the failure of the Crusades.

■ In the absence of central power, local monarchs became powerful leaders. They used nationalism to appeal to the loyalty of their subjects.

17

THE CREATION OF COUNTRIES

By the 1300s and 1400s, Europe was divided into a series of states. The people who lived in them were still subjects rather than citizens.

The great cultural movement known as the Renaissance had begun in around 1250. At the time, only a few countries existed with recognizable borders and government structures. They included France, England, Hungary, Scotland, Denmark, and Norway. The Iberian Peninsula was divided into kingdoms, including the Islamic state of Granada.

COLUMBUS

Christopher Columbus sailed the Atlantic to the Americas in 1492. Although he was from Italy, he went on behalf of the rulers of Spain.

On the Italian Peninsula the largest of the many small states were the Papal States, which were ruled by the pope. Germany, the Low Countries, Czechoslovakia, and Austria included many states ruled by counts, dukes, and princes who came under the rule of the Holy Roman Empire. The Habsburgs of Austria inherited the Holy Roman Empire in 1440, but in 1521 the dynasty split between Austrian and Spanish branches. The Spanish Habsburgs ruled not only Spain but also parts of Italy, the Netherlands, and briefly Portugal, as well as Spain's overseas empire. The Austrian Habsburgs ruled the Holy Roman Empire and parts of Hungary.

Growth of cities

The first challenges to traditional rule came as a result of economic change during the Renaissance. Trade increased and the production of wool and other textiles became **mechanized**.

TIMELINE

ca. 1250
The Renaissance begins in Italy. It is a cultural movement based on ideas drawn from ancient Greece and Rome.

1492
Christopher Columbus lands in the Americas. His expedition is part of a larger European "Age of Exploration."

1521
The Habsburg Empire in Europe splits in two. Its weakness will encourage the emergence of stronger states, such as the Netherlands.

As a result of increased trade, some cities became wealthy and powerful. Citizens began to defy the nobles who governed them. This occurred in the Netherlands and Belgium, and also in German cities in the Holy Roman Empire. People formed **guilds** and town councils in order to set their own laws, free from dynastic rule.

In Italy, wealthy cities became the basis for **city-states** like those of ancient Greece. Cities such as Milan and Padua were home to princes who ruled the surrounding area. The largest states—Venice, Florence, and Genoa—were influential international traders.

To the "New World"

Meanwhile, Europe's influence spread across the globe. In 1492, Christopher Columbus sailed the Atlantic to the "New World." The Spanish set up **colonies** in the new lands he discovered in the Caribbean. Within the next centuries, the English and French had settlements in what are now the United States and Canada, respectively.

TOWNSFOLK

Leading citizens, like these guild members in the Netherlands, began to take control of their towns and communities.

AZTEC

The Aztec recorded their conquest of their neighbors. The inclusion of many defeated peoples in their empire, however, left Aztec rule badly weakened.

←

The European conquest of the Americas was aided by the absence of nations with a strong political identity. A few hundred Spaniards were able to defeat the vast Aztec Empire in just two years. The Aztecs of Mexico had established what seemed like a powerful state, in which lesser states paid tribute to the Aztec emperor, who lived in the vast capital at Tenochtitlán. However, the Aztec Empire included many peoples who had little in common. The Spaniards made **alliances** with tribal groups who resented Aztec rule. The Spaniards and their allies defeated the Aztec in 1521.

WORLD TRADE

In less than 150 years, navigators from European countries opened trade routes around the world. This diagram shows who opened the way to which part of the world.

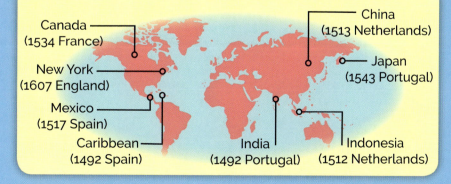

Canada
(1534 France)

New York
(1607 England)

Mexico
(1517 Spain)

Caribbean
(1492 Spain)

China
(1513 Netherlands)

Japan
(1543 Portugal)

India
(1492 Portugal)

Indonesia
(1512 Netherlands)

Around the world

To the north of Mexico, the English, French, and other immigrants met Native American peoples. Native peoples had strong bonds within their groups, but sometimes fought with their neighbors over land and resources, even if the other group shared the same language and culture. Although most Native American peoples had well-defined territories where they lived, those territories usually did not have fixed borders.

Native Americans did not think of owning the land in the same way as Europeans. When the Dutch trader Peter Minuit bought Manhattan Island from the native Manhattan people in 1626, the people simply assumed they would continue to live there. The Dutch, however, saw the island as being their **exclusive** property.

MANHATTAN

The Dutchman Peter Minuit hands goods to the Manhattan people in a deal to "purchase" the island where they lived. This is now Manhattan in New York City.

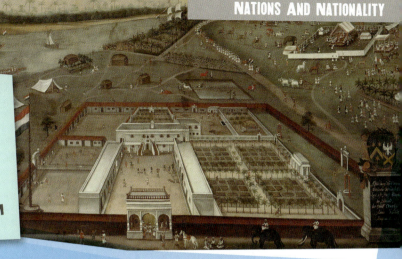

FACTORY

Walls surround a European factory, or trading post, in Southeast Asia. In countries they visited, Europeans began taking over governments to form new colonies.

In the 1400s, Europeans also began to establish colonies in Africa and Asia. The Portuguese set up trading ports in east and west Africa, the English in South Africa and India, and the Dutch in the Spice Islands of Southeast Asia. These Europeans came into contact with many established kingdoms. In the north of India, the Delhi Sultanate—an Islamic dynasty from central Asia—ruled over a majority Hindu population.

In China, strong central governments ruled over a wide range of ethnic groups. In contrast, the islands of Japan were largely ethnically similar. Neither the Chinese nor the Japanese had a high opinion of Europe. They did not believe they had anything to learn from European culture or politics.

IN SUMMARY

- The traditional power of the nobility was challenged by the growth of wealthy cities.

- Trade led Europeans to travel across the world.

- The arrival of Europeans often had a damaging impact for societies in Africa, Asia, and the Americas.

THE NATION– STATE

By 1600, Europe had been split into identifiable countries, but the fate of their citizens was still decided by their rulers.

From the 1500s to the 1700s, Europe was rocked by a series of religious and dynastic wars. The religious wars were triggered by the Protestant Reformation that began in Germany in the early 1500s. Catholic rulers fought to resist the new branch of Christianity.

RELIGIOUS WAR

Catholics in France killed Protestants in the St. Bartholomew's Day **Massacre** in 1572. →

Protestantism took hold in places such as Switzerland, Scotland, Sweden, and the Netherlands. In France, the Wars of Religion (1562–1598) ended in victory for the Catholics. French Protestants, or Huguenots, were guaranteed religious freedom. Nearly a century later, the guarantee was withdrawn. Around 200,000 Huguenots fled from France, mainly to Britain, Ireland, Holland, Sweden, and Prussia.

Breaking Habsburg domination

In the Netherlands, meanwhile, the Eighty Years' War, or Dutch Revolt, (1568–1648) brought together Protestantism with a movement to overthrow Spanish rule. The civil war ended with the division of the Low Countries into the independent Republic of the United Netherlands, which became Protestant, and the Spanish Netherlands, which remained Catholic and under Spanish rule.

TIMELINE

1517
The Protestant Reformation begins in Germany. It sparks two centuries of religious warfare.

1648
The Peace of Westphalia helps to define the nation-state. It encourages the emergence of clearer differences between countries.

1776
Colonial Americans declare their independence and create the United States. The American Revolution encourages similar challenges in Europe.

25

The later part of the Eighty Years' War coincided with the Thirty Years' War (1618–1648). This war began among Catholic and Protestant states within the Holy Roman Empire. It spread until it involved many of Europe's leading powers in the most devastating war fought in Europe to that time. Sweden, the United Provinces, Prussia, England, and Scotland fought the Habsburg Holy Roman Empire, the Spanish Empire, and Hungary. The war helped end Habsburg domination of Europe. The Peace of Westphalia in 1648 gave rulers the right to decide the religion to be followed by citizens in their own territories.

The Peace of Westphalia took an important step in defining nationhood. The rulers of Europe's major powers agreed the idea that a nation-state has **sovereignty** over its own territory and domestic affairs. They said that other governments may not interfere in those affairs.

PEACE

Representatives at the Peace of Westphalia agreed that rulers of a nation-state had ultimate power over what happened inside its own borders.

In addition, the peace established that all states are equal in international law, no matter how big or small the state might be.

Further dynastic wars were triggered by power struggles over the Habsburg lands in Spain and Austria. These were the wars of the Spanish Succession (1701–1714) and Austrian Succession (1740–1748), respectively. England and Scotland were united first in 1603 when King James VI of Scotland inherited the English throne as James I, but the union had little initial effect. It became formal in the Acts of Union in 1707, which created the country of Great Britain.

Revolution!

The dynastic wars were a reminder that few countries yet existed as sovereign states.

UNITED KINGDOM

King James I of England ruled England and Scotland from 1603. The two kingdoms were not united until 1707.

→

CASUALTIES OF WAR

Europe's dynastic wars caused tremendous casualties. No one knows exactly how many people died. These figures are an average based on different estimates.

ca. 2,000,000	Hundred Years' War (1337–1453)
5,873,000	Thirty Years' War (1618–1648)
900,000	War of the Spanish Succession (1701–1714)
ca. 500,000	War of the Austrian Succession (1740–1748)
1,102,000	Seven Years' War (1756–1763)

Much of Europe remained the **fiefdoms** of individual rulers or families. That was about to be challenged. The first challenge came not from Europe but from North America.

Colonial Americans resented taxes imposed on them by the English parliament. Colonists had no representation in parliament. They claimed that it was a fundamental principle of government that they could not therefore be taxed.

In 1775, American complaints turned to revolt. The British Army was sent to suppress the uprising. Although many colonial Americans thought of themselves as being English, they soon realized that they had a chance to create their own country. They issued the Declaration of Independence of 1776, which set the colonists on course to establish their own republic. After American victory in the Revolutionary War, the British recognized the United States of America as an independent country in 1783.

DECLARATION

In the Declaration of Independence, Thomas Jefferson (*standing*), John Adams (*center*), and Benjamin Franklin (*left*) outlined the rights of citizens to govern their own country.

→

GUILLOTINE

The execution of King Louis XVI of France marked the end of the old monarchy. From then on, French rulers would govern only with the support of the people. ↑

French Revolution

In 1789, unrest broke out in France against the Bourbon monarchy. The unrest soon led to a full-scale revolution. The government was overthrown by republicans who began a period known as the "Terror." Huge numbers of the aristocracy, which they called the *ancien regime* or "old regime," were killed. More aristocrats fled to other European countries. In 1793 the revolutionaries executed King Louis XVI and his queen, Marie Antoinette.

IN SUMMARY

■ Religious and dynastic wars rocked Europe. The warfare encouraged the development of national loyalties and patriotism among Europeans.

■ Revolutions in America and France created political and social upheaval in the West.

THE TRIUMPH OF NATIONALISM

The French Revolution sent shockwaves through Europe. It became clear that citizens were gaining power at the expense of their rulers.

The French Revolution ended in 1799. France was now led by a committee including an army general named Napoleon Bonaparte. Napoleon then became First Consul and in 1804 declared himself to be the Emperor of the French. It seemed that the French had simply exchanged one **absolute ruler** for another.

EMPEROR

Napoleon disappointed many people who supported the ideals of the French Revolution. He declared himself emperor of France. →

Napoleon set out to build a French empire that eventually included Spain, France, Italy, the Low Countries, Germany, Poland, Austria, and parts of Scandinavia. He was eventually defeated in 1815 by the combined forces of Britain, Russia, Prussia, and other countries. Napoleon's rule had important consequences for nationhood in Europe. In 1806 he abolished the Holy Roman Empire. In Germany, he created the Confederation of the Rhine, which was the first step to the creation of a unified Germany. In Italy he created the Kingdom of Italy in the north, the first step to unifying the peninsula.

Spreading democracy

The decline in the importance of monarchies continued throughout the 1800s. The new United States was a republic governed largely by an educated elite. Then, in the 1830s, President Andrew Jackson granted voting rights to most white male citizens of any background.

TIMELINE

1804 Napoleon becomes Emperor of France. He builds an empire that spreads across much of Europe.

1914 Nationalist feeling in Europe is one of the main causes of World War I (1914–1918). All sides in the conflict appeal to the patriotism of their citizens.

1933 Adolf Hitler becomes chancellor of Germany. He takes complete power at home as a dictator and expands German territory in Europe.

Changes in voting rights greatly expanded democracy in the United States, although women, African Americans, and Native Americans did not receive the vote. In Britain, the Great Reform Act of 1832 gave the vote to a limited number of male citizens. Further acts extended **suffrage** further throughout the century. A similar expansion of voting rights came in France. The Bourbon monarchy was restored to the throne, but kings such as Louis Philippe ruled only with the approval of the people.

Italy and Germany

Nationalism meanwhile shaped events in Italy and Germany. In Italy, the movement known as the *Risorgimento* ("Rising Again") gathered momentum in the 1840s and 1850s. The states of Italy wished to lose the influence of France and Austria and become united. A campaign led by the nationalist Giuseppe Garibaldi and the politician Count Camillo Cavour defeated the Bourbons and the Austrians to unite Italy in 1861 under King Victor Emmanuel II. The Papal States remained independent, however. The Papal States included Rome, which the Italians wanted as their capital.

DEMOCRACY

"Jacksonian Democracy," named for President Andrew Jackson, gave more male Americans a say in how the United States was governed.

REDSHIRTS

Giuseppe Garibaldi's armed followers, the Redshirts, played a key role in the military campaign to unify Italy. Rome joined the new nation in 1871. →

A similar story unfolded in Germany in the 1860s. Otto von Bismarck was president of Prussia, the largest German state. He used a combination of warfare and **diplomacy** to bring together the former states of the Holy Roman Empire. He created a united German Empire. The new country had a parliament elected by universal male suffrage. However, Bismarck made sure that real political power in the new Germany remained in the hands of Prussia's elite class, the Junkers.

GERMAN EXPANSION

Between World War I (1914–1918) and World War II (1939–1945), Adolf Hitler expanded German territory to include all or part of Germany's neighbors.

GERMANY

Saarland **1935**

Rhineland **1936**

Austria **1938**

Sudetenland **1938**

Bohemia and Moravia (Czechoslovakia) **1939**

Memel, Lithuania **1939**

World War I and political extremism

The creation of Italy and Germany contributed to a general increase in nationalism in Europe in the late 1800s. European powers raced to gain new colonies in Asia and Africa. They made alliances among themselves. Two main allied groups emerged who were roughly equal in strength. The growing rivalries between the different powers eventually led to the outbreak of World War I in 1914. Two cousins, King George V of England and Czar Nicholas II of Russia, went to war against their shared cousin, Kaiser Wilhelm II of Germany. Countries had become very different from the dynastic states of the past.

World War I ended with Germany's surrender in 1918. The peace settlements that followed left many unresolved problems in central Europe. In particular, many German-speaking people became minorities in non-German states. This situation was exploited by the Nazi dictator Adolf Hitler, who came to power in 1933. Hitler promoted an extreme nationalism that portrayed Germans as racially superior to other peoples.

POSTER

This poster from World War I shows the image of the French national hero Joan of Arc. It was designed to persuade American women to buy savings stamps in order to pay for the war. →

EXTREMISM

The Nazis organized Germany society on military lines. Hitler promoted an extreme form of patriotism.

←

Hitler made German society more militaristic as he prepared to free Germans from foreign rule. Similar forms of nationalist thought in Italy, Spain, and Japan led to the development of militaristic, totalitarian regimes.

Meanwhile, in 1922 the Soviet Union had replaced the former Russian empire, bringing together its various ethnic groups in a range of Soviet republics. The only common factor in these new republics was their domination by communism.

IN SUMMARY

■ The rise of popular democracy in the 1800s contributed to a growth of nationalism in the late 1800s.

■ Nationalism was a major cause of World War I. After the war, it was encouraged by extremist right-wing leaders in a number of countries.

35

NATIONS AND GLOBALIZATION

The rise of militarism led in 1939 to World War II. After the defeat of Germany and Japan in 1945, countries began a new type of international relations.

In 1945 the United Nations (UN) was founded as an organization for settling international disputes. To qualify, member states had to be recognized as countries in their own right. They must be self-governing, or sovereign. They must have fixed borders, and organized legal systems and constitutions.

There was a rapid growth in membership of the UN as the empires set up by European powers and Japan in Asia collapsed. From 1947, many former colonies became independent, either peacefully or following a violent struggle. When Britain's colony in India split into the new states of India and Pakistan in August 1947, the Hindu and Muslim populations fought bitterly to gain power.

The Cold War

Meanwhile, new countries such as Korea became flash points in the Cold War. This was an **ideological** standoff between two opposing groups. On the one hand were the capitalist democracies, led by the United States. On the other were the world's communist countries, led by the Soviets. The two superpowers did not fight directly but both supported local wars. Communist forces tried to take over Korea (1950–1953) and Vietnam (1954–1975). The United States led its allies in armed resistance to these assaults.

UNITED NATIONS

The United Nations Security Council meets in New York. It was set up to help maintain world peace.

←

TIMELINE

1945 At the end of World War II, the United Nations is set up as a body to resolve international disputes through diplomacy.

1989 The collapse of the communist states of Eastern Europe destroys the control the Soviet Union has held over the region for over 40 years.

2016 The British public vote to leave the European Union. Americans elect Donald Trump as president after he promises to break up free trade agreements.

The end of World War II left Soviet troops in occupation in most of Eastern Europe. They set up communist governments there. What was called the Iron Curtain divided Europe for nearly 40 years. With Russian support, communist regimes crushed opposing movements until the 1980s. When the Soviet Union could no longer afford to support its allies, however, the communist leader Mikhail Gorbachev signaled that Eastern Europe was no longer a Soviet zone of influence. A series of citizen revolutions saw virtually all of eastern Europe become democratic republics around 1989.

National problems

The break-up of the Soviet Union left the United States as the world's only superpower. It remained the model of a successful nation-state, having survived a civil war and rapid expansion in the late 1800s, and turmoil over civil rights in the 1960s. US power was crucial to supporting other new states. However, many problems remained with the world's nations. States such as Rwanda and Sudan in Africa or Iraq in Asia forced together

KOREAN WAR

US soldiers pose with a captured enemy flag during the Korean War. US forces and their allies fought communist North Korea and China, who were backed by the Soviet Union.

CELEBRATION

Germans celebrate on top of the Berlin Wall in November 1989. Communist East Germany had built the wall in the 1960s to stop its citizens fleeing to the West.

←

different racial or religious groups that simply did not get along. Peoples such as the Kurds in Anatolia and the Palestinians of the eastern Mediterranean were left without a state of their own. Meanwhile, political accidents of the past threw up flash points. The Crimean Peninsula, for example, is part of Ukraine, even though most of its people are Russian and wish to belong to Russia. Russia invaded Crimea in 2014.

UNITED NATIONS MEMBERSHIP

Since its creation in 1945, the growth of the United Nations has reflected the growing number of recognized countries in the world.

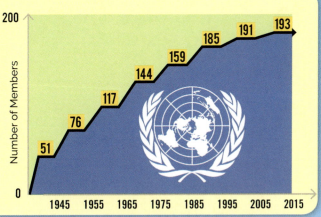

Number of Members

200

193
191
185
159
144
117
76
51

1945 1955 1965 1975 1985 1995 2005 2015

0

After World War II, there had been a growth in international cooperation. In Europe, the European Union was established as a free-trade area in 1993. In North America, the United States, Canada, and Mexico signed the North America Free Trade Agreement (NAFTA) in 1992. However, in the early 2000s, both arrangements faced growing criticism from nationalists. Many people in Europe objected to the freedom of people to move between countries to look for work or to the loss of jobs that were relocated to other countries in the union.

Nations in a global world

Although the nation-state remains the basis of the modern world, it faces many difficulties. The rise of multinational businesses means that economics no longer follow national borders. Companies operate in numerous countries while only paying their taxes in one.

AUTOMOBILES

US automobiles are manufactured in a factory in Mexico. For many US workers left without jobs, moving such jobs abroad was a high price to pay.

BREXIT

These British newspaper headlines reflect the vote in June 2016 to leave the European Union. The decision seemed sure to shake the future of the European Union.

The Internet means that communication and information also flows widely, although countries such as China and Russia attempt to limit access. Together, such processes are known as globalization. A possible threat to nationhood has emerged in religion, as in the attempt by the Islamic State in Iraq and Syria, or ISIS, to form a **caliphate** throughout the Middle East. Such problems as environmental issues, meanwhile, seem beyond the power of any individual nation to solve.

IN SUMMARY

■ The Cold War divided the world into two politically opposed groups from 1945 until 1989.

■ International unions and trade agreements inspired the rise of globalization. The rise was hastened by economic changes such as online commerce, which does not operate within national boundaries.

THE WORLD TODAY

Today most countries are democracies. Communist governments, monarchies, and dictatorships also continue to exist.

North America

NAFTA The free-trade partners of NAFTA generate over a quarter of the world's Gross Domestic Product.

28%

EUROPE In 2016, 28 European countries were members of the European Union.

28

Europe

Africa

South America

SEPARATIST MOVEMENTS

Minority peoples around the world want to create their own countries. They include the Kurds of Turkey and the peoples who live in the Caucasus in Russia. In Europe, both the Catalans of Spain and the Scots of the United Kingdom hope to achieve independence.

BRAZIL Brazil is the only country in South America where Portuguese is the official language. It was conquered by Portugal rather than Spain.

FRAGILE STATES

A fragile state is a country whose central government is so weak that it has little or no control over its territory. Signs of fragility include widespread corruption, a weak economy, and a large movement of refugees.

Asia

CHINA China is the fourth largest country by area, but the largest by population. It has 1.35 billion people, one-fifth of the world's population.

20%

BANGLADESH Bangladesh was part of Pakistan from 1948 until 1971. It won its independence in a civil war against Pakistan.

INDIA The modern states of India and Pakistan were created in 1948. The two nations still dispute possession of the Kashmir region.

TIMELINE

ca. 3200 BCE Organized cultures emerge in Mesopotamia and Egypt. They develop into powerful empires.

800s BCE States begin to emerge on the islands and mainland of what is now Greece. These states are usually based on a powerful city that dominates its surrounding region.

27 BCE The Roman Empire is founded. At its greatest extent, it controls most of Europe, the Mediterranean, and the Middle East.

476 CE The Roman Empire in the west is overthrown, marking the start of a period of widespread population movement.

800 The Frankish king Charlemagne creates an empire that covers much of France and central Europe. The state he creates paves the way for later nations to emerge.

ca. 1250 The Renaissance begins in Italy. The cultural movement is based on the ideas of ancient Greece and Rome.

1337 The Hundred Years' War begins between England and France. The 1300s mark a significant increase in nationalism among Europeans.

1492 Christopher Columbus sails the Atlantic and lands in the Americas. His expedition is part of a larger "Age of Exploration" in which Europeans reach many new parts of the world for the first time.

1517 The Protestant Reformation begins in Germany. It sparks two centuries of religious warfare.

1521 The Habsburg Empire in Europe splits in two. Its weakness will encourage the emergence of stronger states, such as the Netherlands.

| 1648 | The Peace of Westphalia helps to define the nation-state and how countries should interact with one another. It also encourages the emergence of clearer differences between nations. |

| 1776 | Colonial Americans declare their independence and create the United States. The American Revolution encourages other challenges to traditional dynastic society in Europe. |

| 1789 | In the French Revolution, republicans overthrow the French monarchy and execute the king. |

| 1804 | Napoleon becomes Emperor of France. He builds an empire that spreads across much of Europe. |

| 1914 | Nationalist feeling in Europe is one of the main causes of World War I. All sides in the conflict appeal to the patriotism of their citizens to raise forces to fight and money to pay for the conflict. |

| 1933 | Adolf Hitler becomes chancellor of Germany. He takes complete power at home as a dictator and expands German territory in Europe. |

| 1939 | World War II breaks out in Europe as a result of Germany's expansionist policies. |

| 1945 | At the end of World War II, the United Nations is set up as a body to resolve international disputes through diplomacy. |

| 1989 | The collapse of the communist states of Eastern Europe destroys the control the Soviet Union has held over the region for over 40 years. |

| 1994 | The North American Free Trade Agreement (NAFTA) joins the United States, Canada, and Mexico in a free trade area. |

| 2016 | The British public vote to leave the European Union. Americans elect Donald Trump as president after his campaign promises to break up NAFTA. |

GLOSSARY

absolute ruler A monarch with complete power over a kingdom and its people.

alliances Unions between countries for their mutual benefit.

assimilated Became absorbed into a previously existing population.

bureaucracies Government organizations that run a country.

caliphate A large Islamic empire ruled by a caliph.

city-states Political units comprising a city and the region around it.

colonies Foreign territory ruled by a country.

Crusades Religious wars, particularly between Christians and Muslims.

culture The customs, ideas, and behavior of a particular group of people.

diplomacy Peaceful relations between countries.

dynasties Lines of rulers from the same family.

empires Large areas ruled by a single ruler.

ethnic Related to a minority group.

exclusive Restricted to particular people.

extended families Families in which a number of generations live together.

fiefdoms Territories ruled by individuals.

guilds Associations of craftsmen or merchants.

ideological Related to political beliefs.

immigration Moving permanently to another country.

infrastructure The basic structures such as roads needed for the operation of a society.

massacre The murder of many people.

mechanized Performed by machines.

nationalism Feelings of devotion to a country.

nation-state A country that rules itself.

patriotism A love of one's country.

propaganda Material that convinces people to adopt a certain point of view.

resources Materials that are useful.

sovereignty The power of a country to govern itself.

suffrage The right to vote in political elections.

ziggurat A pyramid with stepped sides.

FURTHER RESOURCES

Books

Andrews, David. *Business Without Borders: Globalization.* The Global Marketplace. Chicago: Heinemann, 2010.

Bhote, Tehmina. *Charlemagne: The Life and Times of an Early Medieval Emperor.* New York: Rosen Publishing Group, 2005.

Markel, Rita J. *The Fall of the Roman Empire.* Pivotal Moments in History. Minneapolis, MN: Twenty-First Century Books, 2007.

Nardo, Don. *The European Colonization of Africa.* World History. Greensboro, NC: Morgan Reynolds, 2010.

Sauers, Richard Allen. *Nationalism.* Key Concepts in American History. New York: Chelsea House Publishing, 2010.

Websites

www.good.is/slideshows/ten-lesser-known-independence-movements-fourth-of-july
Good has compiled a list of current independence movements around the world.

www.habsburger.net/en/
"The World of the Habsburgs" is a site about the Habsburg family, whose empire covered much of Europe in the 1600s and 1700s.

https://historyillustrated.org/2016/02/21/nationalism-definition-for-kids/
This *History Illustrated* page features a short video about nationalism and what it means.

http://nationalgeographic.org/encyclopedia/globalization/
National Geographic explains the process of globalization and provides concrete examples.

wiki.kidzsearch.com/wiki/Unification_of_Germany
This encyclopedia entry provides kids with a description of the many steps that helped to create a unified Germany in 1871.

INDEX